YOU VISITED ME

SUSAN HARDWICK

Kevin
Mayhew

First published in 1997 by
KEVIN MAYHEW LTD
Rattlesden
Bury St Edmunds
Suffolk IP30 0SZ

0 1 2 3 4 5 6 7 8 9

ISBN 1 84003 077 1
Catalogue No 1500148

ISBN 1-84003-077-1

9 781840 030778

Cover design by Graham Johnstone
Edited by Michael Forster
Typesetting by Louise Hill
Printed in Great Britain

Contents

ABOUT THE AUTHOR

Susan Hardwick is an Anglican Priest in Coventry diocese. She trained for the ordained ministry at Queen's College, Birmingham (1982-5), since when she has worked for the Coventry Diocese in various areas of ministry. Susan Hardwick was priested in 1994 at Coventry Cathedral.

She is married to an Anglican priest and has two grown-up children.

Foreword

This book is offered as a resource to those whose Christian ministry takes them into the most profound and painful moments of other people's lives. It particularly seeks to address the less often encountered pastoral situations.

This is a privileged place to be, but also very demanding. Those of us called to this task have to be prepared to relate appropriately and authentically to a wide variety of situations; to be able to assess immediately what sort of input is needed and to respond accordingly. It requires us to have fully alert antennae, picking up the signals, attending as much to what is not said and to body language, as to the words spoken. There is no substitute for this personal encounter.

What this book sets out to do is to provide the spiritual resources of prayer, meditation, reflection, words from scripture, and the practical resources of names and addresses of any relevant organisations or associations that may be of help. There is also a service of 'Moving on', to enable the transition to be made between looking back and looking forward. Where appropriate, there are also some practical reflections and suggestions about the particular subject matter, what the visitor might expect to find, and suggestions as how best to approach certain situations.

The prayers are very direct, and seek to stand alongside and to reflect realistically the sufferer's experience. They are 'get under the skin' prayers.

A number of the prayers have been written in the first person so that they have an immediacy when prayed with those in need. If it is felt that the occasion warrants the use of more formal prayer, they are easy to change into the third person as they are being used.

However difficult the situation, and however hard we struggle to find the right words, in the end we need to remember that sincerely stammered, inarticulate expressions of caring carry much more dignity than well-turned phrases slipping too smoothly from the tongue. We also need to remember Jesus' promise given to us in Mark 13:11*f.* about when we are in difficult situations:

'. . . do not worry beforehand about what to say; no, say whatever is given to you when the time comes, because it is not you who will be speaking; it is the Holy Spirit.'

What we need to do is to trust that we will be given the right words, and to open ourselves up to receiving them.

SUSAN HARDWICK

The King will say, 'For I was hungry and you gave me something to eat, I was thirsty and you gave me something to drink, I was a stranger and you invited me in, I needed clothes and you clothed me, I was sick and you looked after me. I was in prison and you came to visit me.' Then the righteous will answer him, 'Lord, when did we see you hungry and feed you, or thirsty and give you something to drink? When did we see you a stranger and invite you in, or needing clothes and clothe you? When did we see you sick or in prison and go and visit you?' And the King will reply, 'I tell you the truth, whatever you did for one of the least of these brothers and sisters of mine, you did it for me.'

Matthew 25:34f

You visited me

Where were *you*, Lord?

Where were *you*, Lord,
 when all this happened?
How could you allow it?

'I?
Yes, *I* was there,
 bowed beneath the mighty weight
 of my cross.
Nailed to the beam,
 at the centrepoint
 of the world's heartache
 and suffering and pain.'

Some words from *Lifelines*, a set of eight small resource books intended for people experiencing particular life situations:

God is always with us. Unseen, unfelt maybe,
nevertheless closer to us than we are to ourselves.
Throughout the Bible, again and again we are
assured of this fact.
'Come to me,
all who are weary and overburdened
and I will give you rest.'

Matthew 11:28

With these words, Jesus assures us of his loving and
constant care, wherever we are and in whatever
situation – but never more so than when life is hard,
when we are in despair, when we cannot go on
in our own strength.

God urges us to be absolutely honest in our dealings
with him: to say it just the way it is, how it feels,
for us.
'My God, my God,
why have you forsaken me?'
Jesus cried out from the cross, at what must have been
the darkest time of his life (Matthew 27:46; Mark 15:34).
His prayer gives us the example, the courage, the openness
to be just as honest about our feelings: to say, to shout,
perhaps to scream, it all just the way it really is.

Lifelines, written by Susan Hardwick, and published by Kevin
Mayhew Ltd. in March 1997, are companion books to *You
Visited Me.*

The eight titles are:

Lifelines for the Stressed, Anxious, Depressed
Lifelines for the Dying
Lifelines for the Bereaved
Lifelines for the Addicted
Lifelines for the Carer
Lifelines for the Unemployed
Lifelines for the Lone Parent
Lifelines for those in Troubled Relationships.

Wideshoes, the Angel, for 8-12 years, is a very user-friendly
exploration of dying, death, bereavement and life hereafter, as
seen through the relationships and adventures of a group of
young angels. Written by Susan Hardwick, it was published
by Kevin Mayhew in May 1997.

PART ONE

Prayers for
particular situations

Abuse

A prayer for strength

Give (N) the strength, Lord,
that she will need
to get through this.

Mental

It has often been said, Lord,
    that words don't break bones,
    as if that was the worst that could happen.
But the truth is, isn't it,
    they can cause even greater damage
    as they scourge the mind
    with wounds that cannot be seen,
    and so are immeasurable.
We pray now for (N)
    who has suffered so much in this way.
Jesus:
    you who knew the barbed words,
    the unjust accusations of those
    who sought to destroy you,
    as well as the cruel taunts of the soldiers,
    surround (N) with your love and your understanding.
Soothe away the bitter hurt.
May she feel valued once again.

Physical: domestic violence

Lord,
    multicoloured bruises
    that are a bitter indictment;
    bearing witness to the abuse,
    the misuse of strength
    against those who are weaker.
Jesus,
    suffering the pain of the vulnerable
    in the scourge, the thorn and the nails,
    may (N) know your strength now.
Give her the discernment to understand
    what action is needed.
Then give her the courage
    to do whatever is required
    in order to change the situation.
Give us wisdom to know how to help.
Her physical bruises will eventually fade,
    but we ask that you will heal
    the hidden and more lasting scars
    of her mind and her heart.

Physical: sexual

Cry of the victim

Dear God!
How *could* he do it?
I feel he not only violated my body,
    but my very soul as well.
There is no place left within me
    that feels untainted;
    no amount of bathing
    that will wash me clean.

Body, mind,
heart, soul;
he invaded them all
and stole everything
that made me feel worthwhile.
Now I feel like nothing – worth nothing.
Oh, Jesus,
Help me!

Prayer for comfort and healing

Degraded, humiliated;
all that was beautiful
dragged in the dirt
of another's lust and evil intentions.
Jesus,
we pray now for (N),
innocent victim
of this most terrible crime.
Gather him up and surround him
with the power and purity of your love.
May it act as healing balm
upon the scars of his mind and heart.

Cry of the parent

Oh, God!
I cannot bear the thought of it!
That beautiful and vulnerable little body
I so reverently, tenderly
nurtured and cared for,
so heartlessly, cruelly abused.
The anguish, the hate,
the rage I feel
is tearing me apart.
For God's sake, help me!

Prayer for the perpetrator

Of all the people, Lord,
    who need our prayers,
    the perpetrator of this terrible deed
    must number amongst the foremost.
You have said that no one, no action,
    falls outside the possibility
    of your redemption.
But it's hard to believe it of this evil;
    harder still to pray for the person responsible.
However, this is what we do now, Lord,
    asking that they will repent of what was done
    – if only so it will not happen again.

Addiction

I'm so frightened

I don't know where or when
   it's all going to end.
I'm *so* frightened.
Dear God,
I need you!

How I used to be – and now

Oh, Lord!
I look back at what I used to be,
   and I look at myself now.
The two don't bear comparison.
What started out as social drinking
   has assumed a life of its own,
     and I don't know how to break the pattern.
Show me, *please* show me,
   before it totally destroys me.

My self-made hell

Dear God,
From the depths of my self-made hell
I cry out to you:
'For Christ's sake, do not desert me!'

A prayer for all who have helped

Psychiatrists and doctors, nurses and therapists,
    and so many others:
    all dedicated to getting (N) better.
Bless them all, Lord,
    for their caring and their skill
    and their total commitment.
But when he gets out of here,
    and they're no longer around,
    then, Lord,
    that's when he will need you
    – more than ever.

You sought and found her

She had lost everything, Lord.
She felt as if she stood at the very gates of hell.
But even there
    you sought and you found her.*
How very much you must love her.
And how very little she feels she deserves it.
But you have proved beyond doubt
    that she is precious in your sight,
    and that you would never let her go.

* Psalm 23 and John 10:1*f*

You raise us up

Heavenly Father,
From the pit of despair
   (N) cried out to you
   and you answered him.
You raised him up,
   and restored him to his family.
'Thank you'
   is too small a word.

A constant God

Holy Lord,
Most holy and life-giving Lord,
Whenever I reach out,
   you are there.
In the midst of my despair
   in so many ways you showed your love,
   and never once deserted me.
In my new-found peace of mind
   you are with me still.
Truly you are a God
   of constancy and commitment.

Carers

You were a carer too, Lord

Why, Lord,
    if you knew you had
    such an important task in life to perform,
    did you not leave home sooner?
Three years out of thirty-three wasn't very long
    for all that you had to achieve.
Was it because you were caring for your mother,
    your sisters and your brothers,
    and would not go until that task was done
    – not even to save the world?
Thank you for that example of constancy in caring.
Help us to be as committed,
    and to get our priorities right.

The perfect Son

Jesus,
    as you hung on your cross,
    your last thought was for your mother,*
    and who would care for her
    when you were gone.
Even at that time of terrible anguish and pain,
    you lived out your son-love to the end.
Help us to love like that.

*John 19:25-27

Guilt and regret

If only I could put the clock back
   and live our life together over again.
I wasted so much precious time
   and so many opportunities,
   and I just did not appreciate him
   – or what we had.
Now those days have gone for good.
All that are left are the memories
   – and such racking guilt and regret.
Lord, forgive me for taking it all
   so much for granted.
Help me to value what is left.

No time

Dear God –
There is just *no* time
   to think of anything
   – other than the next task.
No time to read a book
   – and that includes the Bible.
No time for friends,
   for me;
   – not even for you.
Lord,
   please help me to reorganise my days
   so that I have some time
   for these really important things.

Unjust

Jesus,
   I know it's not his fault
   he's like he is now.
But it's not mine either.
It all seems *so* unjust.

An unexpected treasure

Each small achievement on her part
   – only you, she and I know how hard-won –
   has made me value and appreciate
   the little things in life,
   found in surprising situations and places,
   which formerly I would have passed by
   without giving a second glance.
Thank you, heavenly Father;
   this sensitivity to the hidden beauty
   in your world
   has been an unexpected gift to treasure.

Too much time

Lord,
   (N) is puzzled and confused.
He has longed for the day to come
   when (NN) would be happily settled in a home,
   and he could have some time to himself.
But now that it's happened
   he feels at a loss;
   for there is just too much time,
   and he doesn't know what to do with it all.
Please help him through the empty days,
   until he can see how you want him to fill them.

Death

General comments

Whether the death of a loved one is anticipated and prepared for, or unexpected and sudden, the actual moment of its happening is usually devastating. However foreseen, nothing can prepare those closest for the feelings they experience. Numbless; shock; disbelief; deep grief; anger at God, the doctors and nurses, or at the injustice of it all; feelings of guilt for what was not done for the deceased; denial; relief that he or she is finally out of pain; these are just some of the very usual feelings expressed at the time of death, and after.

They do not happen in any neat order or pattern, for we will each react in our individual and unique way. We have to be gentle with ourselves at this time, giving ourselves permission for these turbulent feelings, which will most probably repeat themselves many times over the succeeding weeks and months, and maybe even years, before we can declare ourselves truly healed.

General prayers

Go forth upon your journey, Christian soul.
Go from this world.
Go in the name of God the omnipotent Father,
   who created you.
Go in the name of Jesus Christ our Lord,
   who died for you.
Go in the name of the Holy Spirit,
   who has been poured out on you,
     and will sustain us both until we meet again.
May God be with you until we meet again.

Cardinal Henry Newman

We give our loved one back to you, O God, and just as you first gave him to us and did not lose him in the giving, so we have not lost him in returning him to you . . . for life is eternal, love is immortal, death is only a horizon . . . and a horizon is nothing but the limit of our earthly sight. Lift us up, strong Son of God, that we may see further; cleanse our eyes that we may see more clearly; draw us closer to yourself that we may know ourselves to be nearer to our loved ones who are with you.

Anon

Fold her, Jesus, in your arms
   and let her henceforth be a messenger
   between our human hearts and you.

Author unknown

Bring us, O Lord God, at our last awakening,
   into the gate and house of heaven,
    to enter into that gate and dwell in that house,
    where there shall be no darkness, nor dazzling,
    but one equal light;
    no noise nor silence,
    but one equal music;
    no fears nor hopes,
    but one equal possession;
    no ends nor beginnings,
    but one equal eternity;
    in the habitation of your glory and dominion,
    world without end.

From a sermon by John Donne

Heavenly Father, help me to remember
in the midst of my sadness and heartache
that neither death nor life,
nor angels,
nor principalities or powers,
nor things present nor things to come,
nor heights or depths,
nor anything else in all creation,
is able to separate me from your love
which is in Christ Jesus our Lord.

Reflections

When day is done,
a figure turns and says a last goodbye.
We cannot understand where they must go, or why.
But as they leave our sorrow
and our sad tears far behind,
they move ahead to seek the peace
that every soul must find.
For now they sail a different ship
upon a different sea –
a voyage filled with love and hope
and new discovery.
And when the journey brings them
to that distant lighted shore,
they'll be greeted by the outstretched arms
of those who've gone before:
people they have known and loved,
and voices from the past
will be singing out the welcome news
that they are home at last.

Author unknown

Death is nothing at all. I have only slipped away
    into the next room. I am I, and you are you.
Whatever we were to each other, that we still are.
Call me by my old familiar name, speak to me
    in the easy way which you always used.
Put no difference in your tone,
    wear no forced air of solemnity or sorrow.
Laugh as we always laughed at the little jokes
    we enjoyed together.
Pray, smile, think of me, pray for me.
Let my name be ever the household word
    it always was; let it be spoken without effort,
    without the trace of a shadow in it.
Life means all that it ever meant.
It is the same as it ever was;
    there is unbroken continuity.
Why should I be out of mind
    because I am out of sight?
I am waiting for you, for an interval,
    somewhere very near, just round the corner.
All is well.

Henry Scott Holland

Comforting words

When death comes it does not extinguish the light of life, for
death is as the dawn, where there is no need of artificial light.

The day of death is when two worlds meet with a kiss: this
world going out, and the future world coming in.

Author unknown

The dead are no further than God, and God is very near.

Author unknown

Prayers

A broken heart

Lord,
    I don't know which is worse:
    that dry-eyed, aching sadness
    or this terrible grief.
I've cried more tears than I thought possible,
    but nothing will wash away the pain of my loss.
My world has fallen apart,
    and taken me with it.
Gather up these broken pieces
    of my life, my heart,
    and graft them into your own.

A wound only you can heal, Jesus

Jesus,
    his passing has left a gap
    as wide as the world.
A place which only you can enter,
    a wound which only you can heal.
Lord,
    please do so now.

Suicide

Dear God,
   I feel so *guilty* I didn't read the signs.
She was quiet, preoccupied,
   but that was all.
I feel so *angry*, too.
How could she do it to herself,
   to me, to the family?
Why did she suffer alone
   – and then leave me
   to do the same?
Lord,
   help me!

Just as we are

Lord,
   we come to you just as we are,
   with no pretence, no bravery.
We lay before you our worries and our fears,
   our grief, our tears,
   and all the pain and confusion
   of these dark days.
Please help us to carry the burden
   and to bear it all.
And may your peace reign
   in our hearts and lives.

The furnace of God's love

Eternal Father,
   gather up the broken pieces
   of (N's) shattered life.
Mould them, shape them
   into something new
   in the furnace
   of your love.

Walk beside me today, Lord

Lord Jesus,
please give me the strength
to face the day
and all whom I shall meet
with a smile and a calm spirit;
to look and to see
with your eyes.
When people stumble out their sympathy,
may I listen with your ears,
and may I have the grace to remember
that they might need comforting, too.
Help me to tread gently
through my world today
– *your* world.
Please will you walk beside me?

Death of a child

Of all bereavements, the death of one's child must be one of
the worst.

It shouts against all that one expects; against the perceived
proper order of things.

Added to the devastating grief, often, are anguished imaginings that their child is 'out there somewhere', wandering
scared, alone and lonely, crying for the parents who are unable
to be there for them to comfort, to protect and to reassure.

Perhaps only another mother can know how particularly
a mother suffers when her child suffers; the child whom she
has carried in her womb and given birth to, how she would
do anything, bear anything, in order to take away her child's
suffering and pain. However, it is important we remember
that the father also suffers acutely and, in addressing the
needs of the mother, his needs should not be forgotten. The

stiff upper lip tradition, 'boys don't cry', the expectation that the man will support the woman, all kinds of social and gender stereotypes, can bring great suffering to a bereaved father.

Bereaved parents, years after the child's death, often speak of their longing to die and to be with their child – even if they have other, living, offspring. This can give rise to dismay and guilt that they are denying the gift of their own life and the value of their other children by feeling this way, and so they may need reassurance on these occasions that such ambivalent feelings are quite natural and normal.

Although each child is loved uniquely, the loss of an only child is particularly traumatic, for a whole world of identity is lost. They are no longer parents with all that involves socially and in the wider community. On an immediate day-to-day basis, huge areas of social contact disappear. No more gathering at the school gate, taking one's turn with other parents ferrying children, and so on. Added to all of this are often guilt-loaded feelings of why it could not have happened to someone with several children.

Why?

Why, God?
Why did our child
have to die?

We hold up to God those who grieve

We hold (N)
   up to you,
   torn with grief
   at (NN's) death.

Comfort them
    in their distress,
    and raise them up
    from the tomb
    of their despair.

The way ahead is dark

Saviour,
    hold our hands.
The way ahead is
    dark.

Why someone so young?

Father,
    why someone so young?
Why not
    one of us older ones instead?
Please help us
    to understand
    and to trust in you,
    in this darkest of times.

The journey back to God is short

Jesus,
    (N) did not travel
    far into this life,
    and so did not
    have far to travel
    back to you.
Hold her in peace
    now and forever
in your everloving arms.

We give our child back to you, Lord

Lord,
    you gave us (N)
    to love and to cherish.
This we have done.
No one could have
    adored him more.
He was our truly beloved.
Now we give him
    back into your care.

She lit us up

Jesus,
    most gentle and tender
    friend of children.
You who valued 'the little ones
    as those to whom the
    kingdom of God belongs'.*
You will understand how (N)
    brought the touch of heaven
    into our daily lives.
She transformed everything
    and lit us up.
Darkness has come upon us
    now that she is gone.
Lighten our darkness now
    we beseech you, O Lord.

* Luke 18:15f

Here for such a very short time

Here for such
   a very short time
   – and then,
   he was gone.
Nothing,
   but nothing,
   will ever be
   the same again.
Thank you
   for those few,
   sweet,
   moments

Help us to forgive you, God

Dear God!
It seems that you gave her
   only then to take her back.
It just seems so cruel and capricious.
Yet, in our calmer moments,
   we know this is not true
   and that we are blaming you
   unjustly for our awful pain.
We need to put the anguish somewhere
   and only you can bear it for us.
Open our minds and hearts.
Help us to understand.

Death of an infant: stillborn or newly born

For God's sake, help us!

Jesus,
    our hearts ache
    fit to break.
For God's sake,
    help us!

Jesus, hold us in our darkest hour

Lord,
    when our child was born,
    we held him in our arms
    and wondered at that new life.
Then we held him in our arms
    and wondered why he should die.
Now all we can do
    is hold him in our hearts.
Ours for such a very short while,
    nevertheless now forever
    enshrined and adored.
Jesus,
    hold us in your arms
    in this, our darkest hour.

Ours for just a few short moments

Father,
    (N); your most precious gift.
So much longed for.
So very little with us.
A few short moments
    which have changed us for ever.
Thank you.

Abortion, miscarriage or termination

For the purposes of this resource book, where space to explore such complex and emotive subjects as these must necessarily be very limited, the whole area of pre-birth death of the child has been explored under three general headings.

ABORTION (FOR NON-MEDICAL REASONS)

The reasons for choosing to have an abortion for non-medical reasons are often many and complex, and the decision is not usually taken lightly. All sorts of considerations most likely will have been taken into account before the mother-to-be and her partner reach what might have been an agonising choice for them.

In recent years, the whole subject of abortion has had a very high profile, with the pro-life and freedom of choice movements representing opposite views.

As Christians, we might well have clearly thought-out views about the ethics and morals of a choice for abortion. However, as pastoral carers, we need also to be able to step outside our own emotional involvement and to lay aside our own particular feelings and conclusions – whatever they may be – in order to help those who come to us for advice or comfort, or both. We need to do this in order to be able to help them verbalise their own feelings of, maybe, uncertainty or confusion, fear, anguish or guilt; to help them work through the reasons for such a proposed course of action and to reach a prayerful decision which is right for them and the unborn child, and then to minister God's healing and grace at the heart of any pain and guilt.

If such situations are not handled sensitively, and any guilt and pain are pushed 'underground', it may be years before those feelings find their way once more to the surface, often triggered by some seemingly totally unconnected event and quite likely displaced on to something or someone else, and having increased greatly in force. Even when the situation *has* been handled sensitively, many women are not fully prepared for what can be a strong emotional backlash to making a choice for abortion.

MISCARRIAGE (SPONTANEOUS ABORTION)

Until the last few years, there was little understanding – except by those who had experienced it themselves – of the great emotional distress caused by a miscarriage. However, whereas formerly, once the physical effects of the miscarriage were over, the woman concerned was expected to carry on as normal, now there is a much greater understanding of the mental and emotional trauma involved for both the mother and the father.

The reality of that little life is now much more often acknowledged and, when possible and appropriate, the foetus is wrapped in a shawl and given to the parent/s to hold and to cuddle. They are encouraged to name the child, thereby giving it an identity and status – no longer 'it', but 'him' or 'her' – and from there on to see that life as an acknowledged part of their family: their first, second or whichever, child.

If wished, photos may be taken of them holding the baby. When enough time has been given to them for this process, they are then encouraged to bid farewell to their baby, allowing the moment to speak to them as it will.

All this allows the grieving process to be healthily facilitated, rather than being buried only to resurrect itself at some future time and place, often seemingly quite unconnected with the event.

TERMINATION (ABORTION FOR MEDICAL REASONS)

On occasion, when the foetus has died in the mother's womb but she had not miscarried spontaneously, or when the mother's life is threatened by the pregnancy for some reason, the pregnancy has to be terminated. Usually, drugs are given that cause the uterus to contract and to expel the foetus.

This distressing and often frightening experience takes place in hospital or at home, depending upon a number of factors such as how advanced the pregnancy is. Larger hospitals have special termination units, where the staff are experienced in dealing sensitively with such patients, and where the mother does not have her distress compounded by being with other mothers who are not experiencing complications and the sight and sound of whose babies crying only serves to emphasise the loss. However, smaller hospitals usually do not have enough demand to set aside such facilities, and the mother has to be treated in the general Maternity Unit. Although the staff try to separate mothers going through termination from the other women, it is obviously difficult.

It's *so* unjust

Oh, God!
I feel so *angry,*
   and *full* of jealousy.
It's so unjust.
Others are still pregnant
   – but I'm not.
Help me!

The hardest thing in the world

Lord,
   it was the hardest thing
   in the world
   to cradle him
   and then to hand him back,
   knowing I'll never
   hold him again.
Take away the ache
   from my empty arms,
   my empty heart.

No chance to get to know my child

Oh, Lord,
   such bright hopes
   dashed so soon,
   with no chance
   to get to know her.
What would my child
   have been like?
What colour eyes and hair?
What kind of nature?
Boisterous and noisy,
   or thoughtful and quiet?
Now I'll never have the answer
   to my questions.
Jesus,
   heal this terrible longing
   and heartache.

Death of a teenager or young adult

Teenager

She stood on the brink of adulthood,
   a rosebud not yet fully in bloom
   and with the potential
   of so much more to come.
A pre-mature flower cruelly cut from the stem.
Lord, can it really be true
   she is blossoming in another place
   and that one day we will see her again?
She was our darling;
   no parents could have been prouder.
Thank you, Lord,
for those golden and magical years.

Young adult

Lord,
    scarcely into young adulthood;
    dreams just turning into concrete reality.
One day here and so vibrant and alive,
    loving and laughing – the next day gone
    and leaving a gap as wide as the world
    in our hearts and in our lives.
Dear God,
    what *is* the point and the purpose
    of such a terrible waste?
Please help us to understand
    and to bear with this emptiness and pain.

Prayer for the school of a pupil who has died

Lord Jesus,
    we are stunned at the loss of (N)
    and as a community we have gathered together
    to share our sorrow, our bewilderment and our pain.
'Why?' is a question we're all asking,
    but there seems to be no easy answer.
We pray now for her friends,
    her classmates, her teachers
    and all who knew her.
We remember her for
    (list some personality traits, etc)
We may not understand, Lord,
    but help us to let go our bewilderment,
    our anger and any desire for revenge.
May our tears be replaced by smiles
    when we think of (N)
    giving thanks for her life
    and all that she was to us.
Help us now to pick up the pieces once again
    and to carry on.

Prayers of a sibling

It's so weird, Jesus –
   there's only me now.
It feels like half of me died too
   and that I've got to be
   both of us to Mum and Dad.
It's really lonely, too.
I miss her so much.
Stay close.
Please.

Jesus,
   I feel really guilty.
We argued so much
   and I teased him so.
I loved him really
   – you know that, don't you –
   and I miss him heaps.
Please give him my love
   – and tell him I didn't mean
   the silly and unkind things
   I said and did.

Death by violence: suicide or murder

It is difficult enough to face, to cope and to come to terms with, the death of a loved one when the cause is accident or illness.

When the anguish of loss is compounded by the knowledge that the life was taken purposefully – by the person who has died, or at the hands of another – extra dimensions are added to the sufferings of the bereaved which are so great as to defy description.

SUICIDE

Religious beliefs

Certain religious beliefs held by the bereaved may have taught them that the taking of one's own life puts that person outside the possibility of eternal redemption. Whereas normally the bereaved with a faith in the afterlife would find comfort in the notion that the parting is but a temporary one, in this situation that now no longer applies so far as they are concerned and believe.

To contemplate that the loved one is condemned to eternal damnation – whatever that may mean to them – not surprisingly gives rise to the deepest distress.

Guilt

There are often the deepest feelings of guilt that signs were not recognised or, if noticed, were not acted upon sufficiently. The 'if only . . .' path is not one to pursue for too long. It is a useful tool to enable the bereaved to ventilate their feelings of guilt, but then it is wise gently to help them understand that, almost certainly, it was a whole multitude of circumstances – many of them probably quite beyond their control, that contributed to making life intolerable for the person who has died, and so they must not continue to punish themselves in this way. It will not bring the deceased back, and the bereaved will need all their inner resources to cope with the consequences of the death, both for themselves and for any others affected who may be looking to them for comfort, support and strength, such as children.

Anger and betrayal

These feelings are quite usual – that the deceased should not have trusted those nearest to them enough to share their anguish; that they suffered alone, and then left their loved one/s to do the same.

Dear God!
How *could* he do it
   – to himself,
   – to me, the family?
I feel so guilty I didn't read the signs:
   – though, *were* there any?
I've racked my mind for clues
   I may have missed.
He was quiet, preoccupied;
   but that was all.
Why did he suffer alone
   – and then leave me to do the same?
Lord, help me!

Of a child

Why *couldn't* she share her anguish?
We are her parents.
Did she think we wouldn't believe her,
   wouldn't understand?
Dear God!
We feel *such* a failure:
   that it was our fault.
When we think of her isolation
   her fear, her pain,
   we simply cannot bear it.
That precious life,
   embodying so much potential;
   how very *much* she was loved
   and how *terribly* we will miss her.
Oh, Jesus!
Help us cope with this unbearable pain.

Now at peace

Now at peace in your nearer presence:
Lord;
    may the misery,
    the loneliness,
    the pain he felt
    somehow find a value.
May his suffering not be in vain.
In some deeply mystical way
    may it be transformed into good.
Take it all and recreate it
    in the furnace of your love.

MURDER

Surely the most dreadful type of death to face is that of
murder.

Surrounded as it is these days by often prurient and
intrusive press and media interest, by the necessary police
enquiries with the constant reliving of details of the last
movements of the deceased; with the dreadful imaginings
of how the deceased must have suffered in their last moments:
their terror and pain – and the knowledge that we were not
there at the very moments in their life when they most
needed us.

The parent/s of a murdered child will feel the last particularly acutely: it is every parent's worst nightmare. It is hard
enough when one's child is ill or in pain and all we can do is
sit alongside, comfort and reassure, and surround that child
with our love. To have been unable to do that at the time of
their most desperate need must be almost insupportable,
and give rise to the deepest anguish and guilt.

As pastoral carers, we come empty-handed to such situations, but with hearts brimming over with compassion, fellow
suffering, and God's love, meeting with the cross of Christ
planted firmly at the heart of the suffering.

Cry of a parent

From the depth of our despair
  we cry out to you, Lord.
Why couldn't we have been there
  in the hour of his most desperate need?
In our most awful imaginings
  we try to picture it all:
    his terror, his loneliness, his pain;
    and we are torn apart.
Yet our pain links us to him
  and to his suffering;
    because of this, it is precious to us.
We just ask
  that you will share our suffering
  as we know you shared his.

Vengeance belongs to you, not me, Lord

Lord,
  you have said vengeance belongs to you.
So help me now to hand over
  this terrible desire for revenge,
  the hate, the pain;
    all that has been tearing me in two
    and driving me insane.
For your name's sake.

Worse than animals

In my very worst nightmares
    I did not dream of this.
How *could* they do it?
Are they animals?
Yet animals kill only of necessity
    and not from evil intent.
Now they are destroying me too
    with all that I feel.
Help me!
Dear God – don't let them succeed.
Help me.

Dying

So soon?!

Lord,
   I knew that, one day, I'd travel this road,
   but I did not realise it would be so soon.
I have so much living left to do;
   so many dreams to turn into reality
   – or even yet to be dreamed.
I had my life so neatly planned
   with every jigsaw piece in place:
   the finished picture would have been
   a credit to you.
But you have chosen
   a unformed lump of clay instead.
Why?

Broken

I am broken,
   Jesus.
Gather me up.
Put me together again.

Despair

Oh, Jesus!
Bad news!
The future looks as bleak and hopeless
   as I feel.
Dark clouds brood above

a barren desert of despair
with only the stark, sharp cacti of my illness
to relieve the landscape.
An empty wasteland
where formerly I saw the ground
as carpeted in green
in which brightest flowers grew,
and overarching all, a sky of vivid blue . . .
Dear God!
Will this darkest night ever turn
back into that glorious day?

Walking with faith into the unknown

The time has come, hasn't it, Lord,
when I must turn
from the anguish of the past
to face the future.
I'm fearful of what it might bring
– but I know I cannot continue
to walk backwards.
Help me to look forward
to what will be:
to walk with faith into the unknown.

An empty cross and an empty tomb

An empty cross and an empty tomb.
Oh, Jesus,
no place could contain
a heart such as yours;
full to the brim and running over,
even bursting open rock
with such amazing love.
How can I be fearful

of what will be,
when love like yours
will catch me up and carry me
through the grave,
and beyond
– to the brightest of futures.

I have said my goodbyes

Loving Father,
I have said my goodbyes.
I have run this earthly race
as best I can.
Now I turn from this life,
to claim the crown
of life eternal.

Watching and waiting with the dying

Suffering alongside

Jesus,
    your mother stood
    at the foot of your cross
    and watched, and waited,
    and suffered with you
    in all your pain and agony.
All she could offer
    was her presence
    and her love.
    (N) is waiting, and watching,
    and suffering

with the person she loves,
at the foot of his cross.
She longs for his death,
    so he will be released from pain
    – but dreads the time
    of their parting.
Suffering Saviour,
    be with them now
    in their darkest hour.

Watching and remembering

Lord,
    we sit by her bedside
    and watch, and listen,
    and think, and remember.
And thank you
    for all
    we have shared.

Treasuring each God-given moment

Father,
    (N and NN) don't know how long they have.
So help them to treasure
    each golden, God-given moment.

Illness

Of a child

I've done all I can, Lord.
Now I have to sit and watch and wait.
I would give anything
   to bear his suffering for him.
I feel so powerless.
Keep me calm, Lord
   so that I can better take care of him.
Please –
   give us both strength
   for the hours and days ahead
Keep him safe
   and make him well again,
   I beg of you.

A child in hospital

Jesus,
   I'm so afraid.
Bring her safely through the operation.
Give the surgeon a true eye
   and a steady hand.
May it be a success
   and may she be home soon,
   fully restored to health.

Soothe away his pain, Lord

Healing Saviour,
  take away his sickness.
Soothe away his pain.
Restore him to health again.

It's over to you now, Father

Father,
  pills and potions
  aren't making her better.
It's over to you now.

Missing

A Child

Oh, Jesus,
   it's the not knowing that's so dreadful.
We hope for the best
   but fear the worst.
Each day that passes
   brings us nearer to despair
   and it's so very hard not to give in.
When and how is this nightmare
   going to end?
Stay very close, Lord,
   we so desperately need you.
   – but stay even closer to our child,
who needs you even more.

Heavenly Father,
   out there somewhere,
   probably alone and very lonely,
   vulnerable and frightened,
   is our child.
Be with her.
Protect her
   and keep her
   from all harm,
   we beg you.

An Adult

Why did he go?
And why hasn't he been in touch?
Has something happened to him?
Dear God,
    the questions run on and on
    through our minds,
    yet we're no nearer any answers.
It's the uncertainty
    that's so very hard to bear.
Be with him;
    bring him safely home.
And be with us
    until that day dawns.
We all so desperately need you
    and your strength.

Prison

The prisoner

Lord,
    I know I did wrong
    and that this is my punishment.
I think of the time still to be spent
    locked up in here
    and it's hard not to give way
    to depression and to despair.
But with your help I'll hack it.
Please forgive me for what I did.
Give me your strength
    to make the best of my 'time'.
Then give me your courage when I get out,
    to make a new life
    that is more worthy of you.

Jesus,
    you who came to set the prisoner free,
    unlock now the doors of my heart
    and let your healing, transforming Spirit pour in.
Forgive me the things that I've done wrong
    and help me to walk a straight path
    from now on.
With you beside me,
    I know I can do it.

The staff

Father,
    in a tough place like this
    it's easy to become hardened
    and to lose my humanity.
Help me to remain compassionate
    and not to abuse the power of my position.
May I never forget,
    even on the most difficult of days,
    that the prisoners are still people
    who bear the imprint of Christ,
    however misshapen they have made it,
    and so to treat them with respect and dignity
    – as Jesus would have done.

The relatives

Jesus,
    these years of separation
    are taking the toll of us all.
It's not just a sentence on him,
    but upon the whole family.
We feel we're being punished
    for the wrong he has done.
Help us to hang on in there,
    and not to despair.
Surround him, surround us,
    with your forgiveness,
    your strength
    and your love.

The partner

Father,
    it's so hard for me,
    but harder still for the kids.
We all carry the stigma, the burden
    – to work, to school, among our neighbours –
    of the things that she has done.
Yet, despite all this,
    we love her still
    and long for her return.
Until that day comes then, Lord,
    please walk this rockstrewn path beside us.
Give us all the courage we need
    and lead us all into a better,
    a more hopeful future.

Psycho-degenerative disease

The gradual loss of a loved one through physical illness is always hard to bear, especially in situations where we are unable to relieve the suffering and can only be alongside, offering our constancy and our care.

We see that cherished person progressively weaken and become more limited in his or her activity, and know the situation will only end in death.

However, there is a particular anguish in watching a much loved one apparently disintegrate mentally and emotionally before our eyes; to see the doors of communication close one by one, and the shutters go up against the windows of their mind and personality; to be unable to know what thinking, if any, lies behind the blank gaze; whether our words hold any meaning for them or, indeed, whether *we* hold any meaning for them; not to know whether they even recognise us as their friend, sibling, life partner or child.

Comparatively little is known about psycho-degenerative disease. Occasional flashes of recognition or of 'normality', when the fog that appears to blanket the mind and brain lifts; a piece of music or words that appear to waken some memory, seem to indicate that some mental processes might well be unimpaired. Expressions of love might be thus recognised even if the identities of those who make them are not; and of course, as human beings, they are still the beloved of God.

God does not see as human beings see; they look at appearances, but God looks at the heart.

1 Samuel 16:7 NJB

Whatever you did for one of the least of mine, you did it for
me.

Matthew 25:40

On the contrary, those parts of the body that seem to be
weaker are indispensable. Its parts should have equal concern
for each other. If one part suffers, every part suffers with it.

1 Corinthians 12:22, 25b, 26

Only a surface covering

Lord,
   I know this dementia thing
   is only a surface covering.
He was such a dear, handsome man
   and, to me, that is how he'll always be.
I see him as he really is,
     deep down,
     as I know you see him.

She understands in her own way

Jesus,
   people say I'm crazy to tell her all the news
   – about everyone and everything;
   they say she can't understand.
But how do they know?
Brains are such complicated things;
   just because one part has gone
   doesn't mean that none of it works.
They say you should speak to people

who are in comas:
so, what's the difference?
I believe that at some deep level of her mind
my words do find a home;
and that she understands in her own way.
Besides which,
it helps me as well
– and that's important too, isn't it.

Relationships

Unwilling to admit a problem

Dear God,
so many things are terribly wrong
with our relationship;
at least, so far as I'm concerned.
But she just won't see it.
She says 'everything's fine',
then walks away from further talk.
What can I do to make her understand
that if it's a problem for one,
then it's a problem for both
– and ignoring it won't make it go away.
Please give me the words I need.

I'm getting better

Thank God
that those swings of emotion,
devastating in their force and violence,
have at last begun to stop.
I'm getting better!

The gap has begun to fill

When first (N) went,
 he left a gap as wide as the world.
But, little by little,
 (NN) has been able to fill it
 in ways she would have thought
 impossible before.
You have been a large part of that.
Thank you, Lord,
 for not deserting her.

Help us to be reconciled, Lord

We've been at war for far too long.
The reason why it all started
 has almost been forgotten;
 buried beneath an ever-increasing
 amount of anger and recrimination.
Forgive us, Lord,
 for what we have each contributed
 to this situation.
Help us to sort it all out,
 to forgive and to be reconciled
 to one another,
 and then to begin again
 with renewed determination
 to do it better than last time.

Stressed, anxious, depressed

Only you can save me

I'm in the depths of a great black pit.
No one can pull me out
  – except you, Lord.
Only you can save me.

Dark clouds

Dark clouds are pressing down on me.
Smothering me until I want to scream,
  and to run away and hide
  from everything and everyone.
Please help me, Lord!
I'm so terrified.

Nothing matters any more

Lord, (N) feels
  nothing matters any more.
That she couldn't care less
  about all that used to matter so much to her.
She is reduced to wondering
  what *is* the point of going on?
Hold her in your arms, Lord.
Raise her up from her despair.

I'm totally wrung out

Oh, God,
   I've cried and I've cried
   until I feel totally wrung out.
I've exhaused my tears
   and my tears have exhausted me.
Now all I can do is gaze
   with dry-eyed sadness
   and an aching heart
   at my situation.

Controlling the situation

What felt like a raging torrent,
   totally out of control,
   has now abated to a river.
Still flowing strongly, even so,
   I now feel more in charge
   of my feelings and responses
   than I have for far too long.
I know there is a long way
   for me still to go.
Nevertheless the healing has begun
   and there is hope
   where formerly there was none.
Thank you, Lord!

Incarnation

A midsummer Christmas Day –
   with roses blooming in the gardens:
   a gift and a sign of your creation.
But the greatest gift
   is the birth of your Son.*
Loving Father,
   may he be reborn now in our hearts,
   our lives.
And may this day
   mark a new beginning.

From darkness to light

Most holy Lord,
from despair to hope:
it's like emerging from a coal-black tunnel
to the light and warmth of the noonday sun.
You turn the darkest night
into the brightest day,
with your healing touch.
We give you thanks and praise.

* Matthew 2:1f; Luke 1:26-2:20; John 1:1f

Unable to pray

Jesus, were you ever unable to pray?

Jesus,
   when you went alone
   into the hills to pray,
   were you ever lonely?
Did you always know
   the presence of the Father,
   – or were there some times
   when he seemed absent
   – even to you?
Did your searching eyes
   scan apparently empty skies?
And when all seeking failed
   did you, like me,
   turn dispiritedly away
   – only then to find him close,
   so close beside you?

Teach us how to pray, Lord

Teach (N) how to pray, Lord,
   with the prayer of the trusting disciple
   who rests peacefully in the darkness
   of their inner self.
Deep down,
   in the centre of his being,
   where you are to be found.
Teach (N) not to pray, Lord,
   when it is your desire

that he merely is;
resting as a child
in his Father's arms.
Desert or town, Lord,
mountain or plain;
you are there before him,
beckoning to him:
Deep is calling
to deep.

Unemployed

'Surplus to requirements'

'Surplus to requirements',
   that's what they said.
Is that the way
   it's going to be
   from now on:
   not needed any more?
Help me, Lord,
   not to despair!

Take my hand, Lord

Take my hand, Lord.
The way ahead
   is dark.

It's been so long now

Father,
   maybe tomorrow my luck will change.
But it's been so long now
   I've stopped holding my breath.
I'll believe it when it happens.
Until then,
   help me not to give up hope.

The same daily round

Jesus,
 each day's the same:
 first the papers,
 followed by the job-centre.
Then it's walking around
 to check out the tips
 on where I might pick up
 some casual work or labour.
Some days I could scream
 with the sheer monotony of it all.
Is it really worth it?
What's it all for anyway?
I'll need your courage
 if I'm to carry on my daily round.

Bad management style

Lord,
 the initial hurt of having to go
 without so much as a farewell 'do'
 – nor even a present –
 has started to fade at last.
I realise now it was not me,
 but they who were at fault.
It was bad management style;
 though that's scarcely an excuse.
I pray now for others' pain,
 caught in the same situation.
Be with them, Lord.
I know how much it hurts
 and how betrayed you feel.

My gifts are free

I never really realised until now, Lord,
    how your status in society
    is wrapped up in your job.
It's so easy to feel like a non-person
    when asked, 'what do you do?'
    – meaning, of course, your paid work.
At first I stumbled and stuttered.
But now I give them a list
    of all the things I contribute:
    my time, my skills, my energy
    – and all for free –
    to those who are in need of them.
These are my gifts to society,
    and I'm proud now to tell of it.
Thank you, Lord,
    for giving me back my sense of worth.

PART TWO

Prayers for any occasion

Protest and pain

Bad things shouldn't happen to good people

It can't be true!
There must be some mistake!
I'm a *good* person.
Bad things shouldn't happen
    to good people.
Why me,
Lord?

Broken

I am broken,
    Jesus.
Gather me up.
Put me together again.

Anger

Dear God!
There is an icy river of anger
    coursing through my veins
    and freezing round my heart.
The intensity of it all frightens me.
I just don't recognize myself
    in any of this;
    I'm a stranger to myself
    and to everyone who knows me.
Please help me!

Fear

Dear God,
Fear frames (N's) life now.
She's frightened to go out,
    and frightened to stay in.
People used to comment
    on how very confident she was;
        but now, she says, they do so no longer.
Where are you, Lord?
Take her hand.
The way ahead seems very dark to her.

Numbness

I don't know which is better:
    that hotpot of emotions
    stewing, bubbling, seething
    – or this numbness;
    this lack of any feeling at all.
At least then I knew I was alive.
But now?
Give me back my feelings, Lord.
I think I prefer the pain
    to this nothingness.

No future

Disillusionment,
    broken hopes,
    dreams that have died,
    reality gone so sour
    that life tastes foully curdled.
    (N) feels there is no future for her

so far as she can see.
She says she wishes she was dead.
Dear God. She needs you!
Give her back her hope.

The furnace

Eternal Father,
    gather up the broken pieces
    of (N's) shattered life.
Mould them, shape them,
    recreate them into something new
    in the furnace of your love.

Dear God, how long?!

How long?
Dear God, how long?!
Will things never change?
However *hard* I try,
    nothing seems to make any difference.
Help me!
For God's sake, help me!

Hope and healing

Lord, you are never apart from me

Lord,
    truly I know
    you are never apart
    from me.
Let me never be apart
    from you.

Jesus, you are everything

Jesus,
    my Saviour,
    my Lord,
    my King.
You are everything
    to me.

You *never* stop thinking of us

When we are downcast, Lord,
    we think of you.
When our hearts are yearning
    for things to be different,
    we think of you.
It's at these times we understand
    that even when we are preoccupied elsewhere
    we are always on *your* mind.
You are greatly to be praised.

Moving on

Thank you, Lord, for moving us on.
For helping us to let go
    of all that bitterness which destroys us,
    even more than does the situation.

Peace, hope and courage

Peace, hope and courage,
    instead of anxiety, discouragement and fear.
This is your doing, Lord,
    and we thank you for it.

The clouds have broken

The clouds have broken,
    and now the sun shines through
    more often than not.
It is your doing, Lord.
You are truly our guiding light!

Moving forward together

Saviour,
    sorrows and joys, laughter and pain
    were finely woven into your earthly life,
    as they are in each of ours.
Because you entered into our world,
    you understand it all from the inside out.

(N's) tears have been your tears,
  as her laughter is yours.
Thank you for this gifting of yourself.
You are (N's) beloved companion,
  ever constant and ever there for her.
Together,
  you will move forward
  into the future.

God of constancy and commitment

Holy Lord.
Most holy and lifegiving Lord.
Whenever we reach out,
  you are there.
In the midst of our despair,
  in so many ways
  you show us your love
  and never once desert us.
In (N's) newfound peace of mind,
  you are with him still.
Truly you are a God
  of constancy and commitment.

Rarely fearful now

Dear God,
That awful fear that framed (N's) life
  rarely makes an appearance now.
Thank you for taking it away
  with your gentle healing touch.

The pieces are one

We read the story of the potter*
   breaking and remodelling his pot,
   carefully reshaping the clay
   until he has got it right.
You gathered the broken pieces
   of (N's) life, (N's) heart,
   put them together,
   and held him throughout the firing.
Now the pieces have been made one.
Thank you,
   tender and healing Lord.

Your light and your truth

Send out your light and your truth;
   they will be our guide
   to lead us to the place
   where you dwell.
We shall hope in you,
   we shall praise you,
   our Saviour
   and our God.

A break in the clouds

I looked up today, Lord,
   and saw a break in the clouds
   through which the sun was peering.
Damp-faced and pale
   and wearing a watery smile
   – yet sun, nevertheless.
Heavenly Father,
   with your mighty arm

* Jeremiah 18:3-4

sweep back the black clouds
that have blocked my view
for far too long.
Let your Spirit shine through
and into the darkened recesses
of my former despair.

A bearer of God's presence and joy

Holy Spirit, you descended as a dove*
upon the head of the Saviour
as symbol of God's
gifting and love.
Sent from the Father
as a sign of his blessing:
truly the proudest of parents
in his 'Most Beloved Son'.
Be a messenger to (N)
from the Father,
a bearer of his peace
and his joy.
Enter into (N's) inmost part
and quicken his heart
with the beat of your wings.

Eternally open wounds

Did the wounds
in your hands and side
ever heal, Lord?
Or will they stay open
for eternity?
By your open wounds,
we are healed.

* Matthew 3:13f; Mark 1:9f; Luke 3:22f; John 1:29f

Little by little

Little by little, Lord,
(N's) sense of utter despair
has lifted.
Now they can see glimpses
of a future and a hope,
where formerly it seemed there was none.
Thank you!

You calmed the storm

Almighty God,
when we cry out to you in our distress
you rescue us.
You reduce the storm to a calm,*
and then you bring us
overjoyed at the stillness
to the shore where we are safe.
We thank you
with all our heart.

It's your doing, Jesus

Slowly I'm pulling my life back together.
The fragments that lay scattered
all over the place
are being reshaped and remoulded into one.
It is your doing, Jesus.
You stooped down to my level,
and gathered me up
in your gently healing hands.
With your loving and tender touch,
you have created me anew.
It is a miracle you have wrought,
and I shall sing your praise for ever.

* Psalm 107:28-30; John 6:16-21

Ready to look forward

(N) is ready, Lord,
  to look forward now
  and not back any more.
She wants to forget
  what lies behind,
  and to reach out
  to what lies before her.
Help her to keep her eyes
  fixed on the future.

The circle has been completed

Where there is Hope
  there is Healing.
Where there is Healing,
  there is God.
Where there is God,
  there is Love.
Where there is Love,
  there is Peace.
Where there is Peace,
  there is Healing.
Where there is Healing,
  there is Hope.
Hope.
Healing.
God.
Love.
Peace.
The circle has been completed.
The end has joined the beginning,
  with God at the very centre
  of it all
  – and of me.
Thank you, Lord,
  for making me whole once more.

PART THREE

'Moving on'

A service to mark the transition from looking
back to looking forward to what lies ahead.
It is designed to be able to be used
in a variety of situations.

Moving on

This is a basic framework. Ideally, it is best to discuss the contents of such a service with those who are going to take part; what elements they would like included – for example: a piece of poetry, a prayer, a reading or a piece of music that is significant for them.

Requirements

- A table, preferably covered with a white cloth
- Two candles per person taking part, one red (or other colour) and one white, each in a holder, set round the edge of the table top
- A larger central candle in a stand representing the Christ-light
- A crucifix
- Flowers and/or greenery scattered around on the table
- Any artefacts chosen by the participants that remind them of the person who has died or which represent the event
- Tape deck or CD player, with appropriate music perhaps chosen by the participants
- A taper
- Matches
- Slips of paper and pens
- Fireproof bowl or dish.

Preparation

Make the table look as attractive and colourful as possible. If possible, place the table in the centre of the chairs to be used. Each pair of candles – one white, one coloured – should be in front of one of the chairs, if possible.

Light the Christ-candle, and the coloured candles.

Turn the music on in time for it to be playing when people arrive.

When everyone is seated, allow a few moments for them just to listen to
the music, and reflect upon the items on the table.
[Words in square brackets refer to particular situations. Use the most
appropriate set.]

The service

Leader   This little service is to mark the turning point between looking back and looking forward. It is a service of 'moving on'.
Not that we expect, or would want maybe, ever to forget, but
there nevertheless comes a moment when we feel we need
gently to close one chapter in our lives in order that we may
begin another.

Of course, the threads of our lives and our experiences
cannot be neatly and tidily contained in clearly defined areas.
Threads of different textures, shades and thicknesses will
escape to trail down succeeding days, months, and perhaps
years – some to good effect, and some not. So we must be
gentle with ourselves when the sad memories and feelings
return, maybe a long way into the future.

Thus, this little service is not a magic wand which will
sweep away painful memories, never to return – to expect
that would be to invite disappointment and frustration.
Rather, it is a declaration of intention and desire to move on.

We are our past – but we are also our future. To move on,
to begin once more to celebrate life . . .

[. . . is to affirm the life of the one who has died.]

[. . . is to say to ourselves that we will not be defeated by
that which has so scarred us.]

When Jesus died on the cross darkness covered the land,
although it was still afternoon. His death left his family, his
friends, his followers, weeping bitterly and inconsolable
with grief. Yet their terrible sadness did not last for ever.
When Easter Day came, and they witnessed the risen Lord,
they realised that when he rose from the dead hope for the
future for each one of us had been reborn.

On the table, are two candles for each of you. One is lit. The other is not. The lit candle represents . . .

> [. . . the earthly life of (N).]
>
> [(name the event).]

The central candle represents the light of Christ.

In a moment, we will have a time of quiet in which to reflect on

> [. . . (name of person).]
>
> [. . . (name of event).]

Here are some slips of paper and pens, and a bowl. If you feel you would like to write down any thoughts or feelings that you wish to lay to rest today – perhaps feelings of anger, despair, or something else – please do so. Then fold the papers and place them in the bowl. When we are ready, we will set fire to them with a taper lit from the Christ-candle, and let them be consumed by the cleansing flame of Love. Or, if you prefer, simply sit quietly for a few moments.

Some soft music may be played at this point.

Leader   Crucified Lord, who took the pain and anguish of the whole world – past, present and future – upon your wounded body, we lay before you our own pain, our despair, our shattered dreams, our brokenness; and we ask you to take them and to transform them into hope and energy for the future. We ask this in the name of Jesus Christ our Lord. Amen.

Light the taper from the Christ-candle and fire the pieces of paper in the bowl.

PRAYERS

Choose from below as appropriate. Perhaps one of the participants, or each in turn, would like to read one or more.

> I am ready, Lord,
>> to look forward now.
> I want to lay to rest

my grief, my despair,
and to reach out to what
lies before me.
I do not want to forget,
but neither do I want
to be locked in the past.
So
help me, Lord,
to keep my eyes
fixed upon the future.
Amen.

The time has come,
hasn't it, Lord,
when I must turn
from the anguish of the past
in order to face the future.
I'm fearful of what it might bring,
but I know I cannot continue
to walk backwards.
Help me to look forward
to what will be:
to walk with faith
into the unknown.
Amen.

Jesus,
when you burst out of your tomb
on that wondrous first Easter morn
– for mere earthly rock could not contain you –
you proved nothing could confine your love,
and that death had lost its sting for ever.
You are our guiding light,

our resurrection hope,
transforming the blackest night
into glorious day.
As I rise from the dark, dead time of sorrow
help me to live the years left fully,
until the day comes
for me to face my own death,
in the sure and certain knowledge
of resurrection to eternal life
– and that I shall be coming home to you,
my Saviour, my Redeemer, my Lord.
Amen.

When first it happened,
I went and stood at the edge of the lake
and marvelled at its stillness;
its tranquillity was so far
from my inner turbulence
that I wanted to ruffle
and disturb its complacency:
to make it mirror the way I felt.
I threw in a pebble
and watched the ripples extend
and extend in ever-widening bands
until they hit the bank,
before returning to the centre.
Then the water was still once more.
And in its calmness and tranquillity
I read your message
of reassurance
and peace
and love.
Thank you, Lord.
Amen.

From the cross
   to the resurrection.
Each has shadowed
   my own experience.
Thank you, Jesus,
   for bearing my pain.
And thank you
   for raising me
   up again.
Amen.

Redeeming Lord,
   you took my pain onto your cross.
And when you rose from the dead
   you lifted me up with you.
You have given me back my life,
   redeemed and renewed.
I will take your gift,
   proffered with open hands.
Help me now to use it
   to your greater glory.
Amen.

Leader We sum up our prayers by joining together in the prayer which Jesus himself taught us. We will use the traditional version.

All Our Father, which art in heaven, hallowed be thy name. Thy kingdom come. Thy will be done, on earth, as it is in heaven. Give us this day our daily bread. Forgive us our trespasses, as we forgive those who trespass against us. Lead us not into temptation, but deliver us from evil. For thine is the kingdom, the power and the glory, for ever and ever. Amen.

SUGGESTED BIBLE READINGS

When I was in great need, the Lord saved me.
Be at rest once more, O my soul.

Psalm 116:6b, 7a

Blessed are those who mourn,
for they will be comforted.

Matthew 5:4

One day Jesus said to his disciples, 'Let's go over to the other side of the lake.' So they got into a boat and set out, and as they sailed he fell asleep. A squall came down on the lake so that the boat was being swamped, and they were in great danger. The disciples went and woke him, saying, 'Master! Master! We are going to drown!' He got up and rebuked the wind and the raging waters; and all was calm.

Luke 8:22f

They cried out to God in their trouble
and he brought them out of their distress.
He stilled the storm to a whisper . . .
and he guided them to their desired haven.

Psalm 107:28-30

Jesus came and stood among them and said,
'Peace be with you!'

John 20:19b

God will wipe every tear from their eyes;
there will be no more death,
or mourning or crying or pain,
for the old order of things has passed away.

Revelation 2 1:4

Light the white candle of each pair from the Christ-candle.

Leader   These candles that have just been lit represent . . .

[. . . the new life of (N), and of each of us.]

[our own resurrection from the dead, dark time of the past months.]

When you are ready, blow out your coloured candle, leaving the white one lit.

Appropriate music may be played in the background.

When all the coloured candles are blown out, one of the following prayers may be appropriate.

Father,
we give our loved one back to you and,
just as you first gave him to us
and did not lose him in the giving,
so we have not lost him in returning him to you.

Lift us up that we may see further,
beyond the horizon of our grief and loss,
to the life we have yet to live.
Take our hand, Lord, and lead us on.
Amen.

1st verse 'anon'; 2nd verse, the author

If appropriate, invite the participant/s to read this. Otherwise substitute names in place of pronouns.

Father, I give my suffering to you. Only you know the entirety of the anguish that has been mine these past months. Take the pain, Lord; the dark memories, the nightmare of what happened, which seems to have entered and tainted my very soul.

Lift me up so that I may see further, beyond the horizon of my grief and loss, to the life I have yet to live. Take my hand, Lord, and lead me on into the beckoning future. Amen.

Leader   Our time together may have given rise to thoughts and feelings which you would like to share. If that is the case, please feel free to do so now.

Allow time for the sharing of thoughts and feelings.

Leader   When you are ready, extinguish your white candle, in the knowledge that its fire of hope burns now in your mind and your heart.

Wait until all candles have been extinguished.

Leader   I extinguish the Christ-candle.

But his love burns on in our minds, our hearts and our lives, lighting up the darkest places, and dispelling all that holds us captive. Thanks be to God. Amen.

At the beginning, I said this little service was not a magic wand which will sweep away painful memories, never to return. But I do hope that it has brought you peace and healing and hope. Now we set out on this next stage of the journey, in the sure knowledge that we do not walk alone, using this beautiful and ancient prayer of journeying.

Jesus:

may all that is you flow into me.

May your body and blood be my food and drink.

May your passion and death be my strength and life.

Jesus:
  with you by my side, enough has been given.
May the shelter I seek be the shadow of your cross.
Let me not run from the love which you offer;
  but hold me safe from the forces of evil.
On each of my dyings shed your light and your love.
Keep calling to me until that day comes when,
  with all your saints,
I may praise you for ever.
Amen.

'Soul of Christ' The Spiritual Exercise: A Literal Translation and a Contemporary Reading by David L. Fleming, S.J. (The Institute of Jesuit Sources, 1987.)

Prayer of blessing

God the Father, beyond and yet within all of your Creation; God the Son, walking in front and yet beside; God the Holy Spirit, descending and comforting; weave your threefold peace and love throughout our hearts and our lives. And may the blessing of God Almighty, the Father, the Son and the Holy Spirit, rest upon you, and remain with you, now and always. Amen.

PART FOUR

Words from Scripture

The Old Testament

Genesis

The Lord said, 'I am with you and will watch over you wherever you go'.

Genesis 28:15a

Leviticus

I will walk among you and be your God,
and you will be my people.

Leviticus 26:12

Samuel

God does not see as human beings see; they look at appearances, but God looks at the heart.

1 Samuel 16:7b NJB

The Psalms

The Lord is a refuge for the oppressed, a stronghold in times of trouble.
    Those who know your name will trust in you, for you, Lord, have never forsaken those who seek you.

Psalm 9:9, 10

Even though I walk through the valley of the shadow of death, I will fear no evil, for you are with me.
Your rod and staff, they comfort me.

Psalm 23:4

Encourage me to walk in your truth and teach me, since you are the God who saves me.

Psalm 25:5 NJB

Put your hope in God, be strong, let your heart be bold, put your hope in God.

Psalm 27:14 NJB

The Lord is my strength and my shield; my heart trusts in him, and I am helped.

Psalm 28:7a

Be strong and take heart, all you who hope in the Lord.

Psalm 31:24

The Lord is close to the broken-hearted, and saves those who are crushed in spirit.

Psalm 34:18

Lord, all my longing is known to you, my sighing no secret from you, my heart is throbbing, my strength has failed, the light has gone out of my eyes.

Psalm 38:9, 10 NJB

I waited patiently for the Lord; he turned to me and heard my cry.

He lifted me out of the slimy pit, out of the mud and mire; he set my feet on a rock and gave me a firm place to stand. He put a new song in my mouth.

Psalm 40:1, 2, 3a

You, God, have not withheld your tenderness from me; your faithful and steadfast love will always guard me.

Psalm 40:11 NJB

Yet I am poor and needy; may the Lord think of me.
You are my help and my deliverer; O my God, do not delay.

Psalm 40:17

The Lord will sustain him on his sickbed, and restore him from his bed of illness.

Psalm 41:3

Why are you so downcast, O my soul? Why so disturbed within me?
Put your hope in God.

Psalm 42:5a

Deep calls to deep.

Psalm 42:7a

Send forth your light and your truth, let them guide me; let them bring me to your holy mountain, to the place where you dwell.

Psalm 43:3

God is our refuge and strength, an ever-present help in trouble.
Therefore we will not fear, though the earth give way, though mountains fall into the heart of the sea, and its waters roar and foam, and the mountains quake with their surging.

Psalm 46:1-3

Be still, and know that I am God. I will be exalted among the nations, I will be exalted in the earth.

Psalm 46:10

Cast your cares on the Lord and he will sustain you.

Psalm 55:22a

When I am afraid, I will trust in you.

Psalm 56:3

Hear my cry, O God; listen to my prayer.
From the ends of the earth I call to you, I call as my heart grows faint; lead me to the rock that is higher than I.
For you have been my refuge, a strong tower against the foe. I long to dwell in your tent for ever and take refuge in the shelter of your wings.

Psalm 61:1-4

Save me, God, for the waters have closed in on my very being.

I am sinking in the deepest swamp and there is no firm ground.

I have stepped into deep water and the waves are washing over me.

I am exhausted with calling out, my throat is hoarse, my eyes are worn out with searching for my God.

Psalm 69:1-3 NJB

Be my rock of refuge, to which I can always go; give the command to save me, for you are my rock and my fortress.

Psalm 71:3

God says, 'I removed the burden from their shoulders . . . In your distress, you called and I rescued you, I answered you out of a thundercloud.'

Psalm 81:6a, 7a

O Lord, the God who saves me, day and night I cry out before you. May my prayer come before you, turn your ear to my cry. For my soul is full of trouble . . .

Psalm 88:1-3a

I will say of the Lord, 'He is my refuge and my fortress, my God in whom I trust.' You will not fear the terror of the night, nor the arrow that flies by day.

For he will command his angels concerning you to guard you in all your ways; they will lift you up in their hands, so that you will not strike your foot against a stone.

'Because he loves me,' says the Lord, 'I will rescue him; I

will protect him for he acknowledges my name. He will call upon me, and I will answer him; I will be with him in trouble.'

Psalm 91:2, 5, 11, 12, 14, 15a

When I said, 'My foot is slipping', your love, O Lord, supported me.
    When anxiety was great within me, your consolation brought joy to my soul.

Psalm 94:18, 19

The Lord has become my fortress, and my God the rock in whom I take refuge.

Psalm 94:22

They cried out to the Lord in their trouble, and he brought them out of their distress.
    He stilled the storm to a whisper; the waves of the sea were hushed . . . and he guided them to their desired haven.

Psalm 107:28-30

When I was brought low, God gave me strength. My heart, be at peace once again.

Psalm 116:6b, 7a NJB

In my anguish I cried to the Lord, and he answered by setting me free. The Lord is with me; I will not be afraid.

Psalm 118:5, 6a

My comfort in my suffering is this: your promise preserves my life.

Psalm 119:50

I lift up my eyes to the hills – where does my help come from? My help comes from the Lord, the Maker of heaven and earth.

He will not let your foot slip – he who watches over you will not slumber; indeed, he who watches over Israel will neither slumber nor sleep.

The Lord watches over you – the Lord is your shade at your right hand; the sun will not harm you by day nor the moon by night.

The Lord will keep you from all harm – he will watch over your life; the Lord will watch over your coming and going both now and for evermore.

Psalm 121:1-8

I will praise you, O Lord, with all my heart. When I called you answered me.

Psalm 138:1a, 3a

Though I walk in the midst of trouble you preserve my life . . . with your right hand you save me.

Psalm 138:7

O Lord, you have searched me and you know me. . . . you perceive my thoughts from afar.

If I rise on the wings of the dawn, if I settle on the far side of the sea, even there your hand will guide me, your right hand will hold me fast.

If I say, 'Surely the darkness will hide me and the light

become night around me', even the darkness will not be darkness to you; the night will shine like the day, for darkness is as light to you.

For you created my inmost being; you knit me together in my mother's womb. My frame was not hidden from you when I was made in the secret place.

How precious to me are your thoughts, O God! How vast is the sum of them! When I am awake I am still with you.

Search me, O God, and know my heart; test me, and know my anxious thoughts. See if there is any offensive way in me, and lead me in the way everlasting.

Psalm 139:1, 2b, 9-13, 15a, 17, 18b, 23, 24

Listen to my cry, for I am in desperate need.

Psalm 142:6a

I have put my trust in you. Show me the way I should go, for to you I lift up my soul.

Psalm 143:8b

Reach down your hand from on high; deliver me and rescue me from the mighty waters.

Psalm 144:7a

The Lord lifts up all who are bowed down.

Psalm 145:14b

The Lord is near to all who call on him.

Psalm 145:18a

Proverbs

Commend what you do to God, and your plan will be achieved . . . The human heart may plan a course, but it is God who makes the steps secure.

Proverbs 16:3, 9 NJB

Isaiah

Lord, you have been a refuge for the poor, a refuge for the needy in distress, a shelter from the storm and shade from the heat.

Isaiah 25:4a

Do not fear, for I am with you; do not be dismayed, for I am your God. I will strengthen you and help you; I will uphold you with my righteous right hand.

Isaiah 41:10

When you pass through the waters, I will be with you; and when you pass through the rivers, they will not sweep over you.
   When you walk through the fire, you will not be burned; the flames will not set you ablaze.
   For I am the Lord, your God, the Holy One of Israel, your Saviour.

Isaiah 43:2, 3a

Even to your old age and grey hairs I am he. I am he who will sustain you. I have made you, and I will carry you; I will sustain you and I will rescue you.

Isaiah 46:4

In all their distress he too was distressed, and the angel of his presence saved them. In his love and mercy he redeemed them; he lifted them up and carried them.

Isaiah 63:9

As a mother comforts her child, so will I comfort you.

Isaiah 66:13a

Jeremiah

Blessed is anyone who trusts in God . . . Such a person is like a tree by the waterside that thrusts its roots to the stream: when the heat comes it has nothing to fear.

Jeremiah 17:7, 8a NJB

Jonah

When my life was ebbing away, I remembered you, Lord, and my prayer rose to you.

Jonah 2:7a

The New Testament

Matthew

Jesus said, 'Blessed are those who mourn: for they will be comforted.'

Matthew 5:4

The King will reply, 'Whatever you did for one of the least of mine, you did it for me.'

Matthew 25:40 – Author's adaptation

Jesus said, 'Look, I am with you always; yes, to the end of time.'

Matthew 28:20b NJB

Luke

When the Lord saw her, his heart went out to her and he said, 'Don't cry'.

Luke 7:13

Jesus said, 'The Son of man came to seek and to save what was lost.'

Luke 19:10

John

God so loved the world that he gave his one and only Son, so that whoever believes in him shall not perish but have eternal life.

John 3:16

If the Son sets you free, you will be free indeed.

John 8:36

Jesus said, 'Do not let your hearts be troubled. Trust in God; trust also in me.'

John 14:1

Jesus said, 'In my Father's house are many rooms; if it were not so, I would have told you. I am going there to prepare a place for you.'

John 14:2

Jesus said, 'Peace I leave with you; my peace I give you. I do not give to you as the world gives. Do not let your hearts be troubled and do not be afraid.'

John 14:27

Jesus said, 'In me you may have peace. In this world you will have trouble. But take heart! I have overcome the world.'

John 16:33

Jesus came and stood among them and said, 'Peace be with you!'
John 20:19b

Romans

Suffering produces perseverance; perseverance, character; and character, hope. And hope does not disappoint us, because God has poured out his love into our hearts by the Holy Spirit, whom he has given us.

Romans 5:3b, 4, 5

Corinthians

So, whether you eat or drink or whatever else you do, do it all for the glory of God. Do not cause anyone to stumble.

1 Corinthians 10:31, 32a

Those parts of the body that seem to be weaker are indispensable . . . there should be no division in the body, but its parts should have equal concern for each other. If one part suffers, every part suffers with it.

1 Corinthians 12:22, 25, 26a

Praise be to the God and Father of our Lord Jesus Christ, the Father of compassion and the God of all comfort, who comforts us in all our troubles. For just as the sufferings of Christ flow over into our lives so also through Christ our comfort overflows.

2 Corinthians 1:3, 4a, 5

We are hard pressed on every side, but not crushed; perplexed, but not in despair.

2 Corinthians 4:8

Therefore we do not lose heart. Though outwardly we are wasting away, yet inwardly we are being renewed day by day. So we fix our eyes not on what is seen, but on what is unseen. For what is seen is temporary, but what is unseen is eternal.

2 Corinthians 4:16, 18

God, who comforts the downcast . . .

2 Corinthians 7:6a

Paul said, 'Three times I pleaded with the Lord to take my thorn in the flesh away from me. But he said to me, 'My grace is sufficient for you, for my power is made perfect in weakness.'

Therefore I will boast all the more gladly about my weaknesses, so that Christ's power may rest on me.'

2 Corinthians 12:8, 9

Ephesians

Paul said, 'I kneel before the Father, from whom his whole family in heaven and on earth, derives its name.

'I pray that out of his glorious riches he may strengthen you with power through his Spirit in your inner being, so that Christ may dwell in your hearts through faith.

'And I pray that you, being rooted and established in love, may have power, together with all the saints, to grasp how

wide and long and high and deep is the love of Christ, and
to know this love that surpasses knowledge – that you may
be filled to the measure of all the fulness of God.'

Ephesians 3:14-19

Do not get drunk on wine . . . Instead, be filled with the Spirit.

Ephesians 5:18

Philippians

The Lord is near. Do not be anxious about anything, but in
everything, in prayer and petition, with thanksgiving, present your requests to God. And the peace of God, which
transcends all understanding, will guard your hearts and
your minds in Christ Jesus.

Philippians 4:5b-7

Colossians

Whatever you do, work at it with all your heart, as working
for the Lord.

Colossians 3:23

Thessalonians

For those who sleep, sleep at night, and those who get drunk,
get drunk at night. But since we belong to the day, let us be
self-controlled, putting on faith and love as a breastplate,
and the hope of salvation as a helmet.

1 Thessalonians 5:7, 8

May our Lord Jesus Christ himself and God our Father who loved us and by his grace gave us eternal encouragement and good hope, encourage your hearts and strengthen you in every good deed and word.

2 Thessalonians 2:16, 17

Peter

People are slaves to whatever has mastered them.

2 Peter 2:19b – adapted by author

Revelation

Jesus said, 'Look, I am standing at the door, and knocking. If one of you hears me calling and opens the door, I will come in and share a meal at that person's side.'

Revelation 3:20 NJB

Then I saw a new heaven and a new earth; the first heaven and the first earth had disappeared now, and there was no longer any sea.

I saw the Holy City, the new Jerusalem, coming down out of heaven from God, prepared as a bride dressed for her husband.

Then I heard a loud voice call from the throne, 'Look, here God lives with human beings. He will make his home among them; they will be his people, and he will be their God, God-with-them.

'He will wipe away all tears from their eyes; there will be no more death, and no more mourning or sadness or pain.

The world of the past has gone.' Then the One sitting on the throne spoke. 'Look, I am making the whole of creation new.'

Revelation 21:1-5a NJB

God said, 'I am the Alpha and the Omega, the Beginning and the End. I will give water from the well of life free to anybody who is thirsty.'

Revelation 21:6b NJB

PART FIVE

Resources

Resources

Government departments and organisations

Department of Health: Richmond House, 79 Whitehall, London SW1A 2NS Tel: 0171 210 3000

Mental Health and NHS Community Care Division: Wellington House, 133-155 Waterloo Road, London SE1 8UG Tel: 0171 972 2000

Home Office: 50 Queen Anne's Gate, London SW1H 9AT Tel: 0171 273 4000

The Benefits Agency: Quarry House, Quarry Hill, Leeds LS2 7UA Tel: 0113 232 4000

The Welsh Office: New Crown Buildings, Cathays Park, Cardiff CF1 3NQ Tel: 01222 825111

The Scottish Office: New St Andrew's House, St James Centre, Edinburgh EH1 3TG Tel: 0131 244 5151

General

British Association for Sexual and Marital Therapy: PO Box 62, Sheffield S10 3TS

British Red Cross Society: 9 Grosvenor Crescent, London SW1 7EJ Tel: 0171 235 5454

Carers National Association: Head Office, 20-25 Glasshouse Yard, London EC1A 4JS Tel: 0171 490 8818, Carersline: 0171 490 8898 (Mon-Fri, 1-4 pm)

Catholic Housing Aid Society: 189a Old Brompton Road, London SW5 0AR Tel: 0171 373 4961

Catholic Marriage Advisory Centre: 1 Blythe Mews, Blythe Road, London W14 0NW Tel: 0171 371 1341

Church Army: Headquarters, Independents Road, Blackheath, London SE3 9LG Tel: 0181 318 1226

Citizens Advice Bureau (National Association): 115-123 Pentonville Road, London N1 9LZ Tel: 0131 657 2000

The Compassionate Friends: 53 North Street, Bristol BS3 1EN Tel: Helpline 0117 953 9639, Admin: 0117 966 5202, Fax: 0117 966 5202
Friendship and understanding for bereaved parents whose children have died at any age and from any cause

Crossroads Care Schemes Ltd: 10 Regent Place, Rugby, Warwickshire CV21 2PN Tel: 01788 573653

Cruse Bereavement Care (Branches Nationwide): National Office: Cruse House, 126 Sheen Road, Richmond, Surrey TW9 1UR Tel: 0181 940 4818
Counselling and advice for all bereaved people

Holiday Care Service: 2 Old Bank Chambers, Station Road, Horley, Surrey RH6 9HW Tel: 01293 774535
Information/support re holidays for people with low income or special needs

Joint Council for the Welfare of Immigrants: 115 Old Street, London EC1V 9JR Tel: 0171 251 8706 (Helpline 2-5 pm Mon/Tues/Thurs)

Missing Person Bureau: Roebuck House, 284-6 Richmond House West, London SW14 7JE Tel: 0181 392 2000

Ockenden Venture: Constitution Hill, Woking, Surrey, GU22 7UU Tel: 01483 772012/3
Help for refugees

Refugee Support Centre: King George's House, Stockwell Road, London, SW9 9ES Tel: 0171 733 1482
Counselling; advice to professionals

Relate (Marriage Guidance): Herbert Gray College, Little Church Street, Rugby, CV21 3AP Tel: 01788 573241, Fax: 01788 535007

Salvation Army Social Services: 105-109 Judd Street, King's Cross, London WC1H 9TS Tel: 0171 383 4230, Fax: 0171 383 2562
An international Christian movement. Areas of work:
- *Alcoholism assessment, treatment and rehabilitation*
- *Community homes for children and adolescents, plus residential hostels for young people*
- *Day care centres for various classes of needy people*
- *Elderly people's homes and sheltered housing*
- *Hostels for the single homeless and for families*
- *Prison visiting, family welfare and aftercare*
- *Family Tracing Service: Address as above, Tel: 0171 383 2772*

Counselling Service: 18 Thanet Street, London, WC1H 9QL Tel: 0171 383 4822

Samaritans: Tel: 0345 909090
A listening ear, any time, 365 days of the year, for the price of a local call

Shelter: 88 Old Street, London EC1V 9HU
Tel: 0171 253 0202

Social Care Association: 23a Victoria Road, Surbiton, Surrey KT6 4JZ Tel: 0181 390 6831

Terence Higgins Trust: BM Aids, London WC1N 3XX
Tel: 0171 831 0330

Victims of Crime: St. Leonard's, Nuttall Street, London
N1 5LZ Tel: 0171 729 1226

Victim Support: National Office, Cranmer House,
39 Brixton Road, London SW9 6DZ Tel: 0171 735 9166

Women's Health: 52 Featherstone Street, London
EC1Y 8RT Tel: 0171 251 6580 Fax: 0171 608 0928
National Information Service

Women's Therapy Centre: 6/9 Manor Gardens, London
N7 6LA Tel: 0171 263 6200, Fax: 0171 281 7879
Advice and information service

WRVS: 234-244 Stockwell Road, London SW9 9SP
Tel: 0171 416 0146

Children and families

For associations, etc, concerned with various marital thera-
pies, see also General Section.

Action for Sick Children: Argyle House, 29-31 Euston
Road, London NW1 2SD Tel: 0171 833 2041
National Association for the welfare of children in hospital

Anti-Bullying Campaign: 10 Borough High Street, London
SE1 9QQ Tel: 0171 378 1446

Barnardos: Contact nearest regional office
Services include:
• *working with children and families through 160 local projects*
• *support for families under stress*
• *help for young people with learning disabilities to live and
  work in the community*
• *day centres for under-fives who may be at risk*

- *residential provision for young people with behavioural problems, severe physical or learning disabilities*
- *support for children and families affected by HIV/AIDS, homeless young people and those who have been sexually abused.*
- *working partnership with parents, local authorities, churches and other agencies*
- *holidays*

Child Poverty Action Group: 1-5 Bath Street, London EC1V 9PY Tel: 0171 253 3406

Childline: 2nd Floor, Royal Mail Building, Studd Street, London N1 0QW or Freepost, 1111, London N1 0BR Tel: 0171 239 1000, Freephone: 0800 1111

Childline (Scotland): 18 Albion Street, Glasgow G1 1LH or Freepost, 1111, Glasgow G1 4BR Tel: 0141 552 1123, Freephone: 0800 1111

Children's Legal Centre: 20 Compton Terrace, London N1 2UN Tel: 0171 359 6251

Christian Family Concern: Wallis House, 42 South Park Hill Road, South Croydon CR2 7YB Tel: 0181 688 0251/0018

Family Holiday Association: 16 Mortimer Street, London W1N 7RD Tel: 0181 349 4044

(National) Association of Family Mediation and Conciliation Services: 50 Westminster Bridge Road, London SE1 7QY Tel: 0171 721 7658

Association for Family Therapy: c/o Pauline Jenkins, 6 Heol Seddon, Danscroft, Llandaff, Cardiff CF5 2GX

Family Welfare Association: 501-5 Kingsland Road, Dalston, London E8 4AU Tel: 0171 254 6251

Gingerbread: 16-17 Clerkenwell Close, London EC1R 0AA
Tel: 0171 336 8183, Fax: 0171 336 8185,
Helpline: 0171 336 8184
Single parent support group

Holiday Care Service: 2 Old Bank Chambers, Station Road,
Horley, Surrey RH6 9HW Tel: 01293 774535
Information and advice for people with low income/special needs

MATCH (Mothers Apart from Their Children):
BM Problems, WC1N 3XX

Mothers Union: 24 Tufton Street, London SW1P 3RB
Tel: 0171 222 5533

Network of Access and Child Contact Centres: St
Andrews United Reformed Church, Goldsmith Street,
Nottingham, NG1 5JT Tel: 0115 948 4557

National Children's Bureau: 8 Wakley Street, Islington,
London EC1V 7QE Tel: 0171 278 9441

National Family Mediation: 9 Tavistock Place, London
WC1H 9SN Tel: 0171 383 5993

National Stepfamily Association: Chapel House,
18 Hatton Place, London EC1N 8RU Tel: 0171 208 2460,
Helpline: 0990 168 388 (2-5pm, 7-10pm weekdays)

National Council for One Parent Families: 255 Kentish
Town Road, London NW5 2LX Tel: 0171 267 1361

NCH – Action for Children: 85 Highbury Park, London
N5 1UD Tel: 0171 226 2033
17 Newton Place, Glasgow G3 7PY Tel: 0141 332 4041

**NORCAP (National Association for the Counselling of
Adoptees and Parents):** 112 Church Road, Wheatley,

Oxfordshire OX33 1LU   Tel: 01865 875000,
Fax: 01865 875686

NSPCC (National Society for the Prevention of Cruelty to Children): National Centre: 42 Curtain Road, London EC2A 3NH   Tel: 0171 825 2500

NSPCC Child Protection Helpline: 0800 800 500
National free 24-hour telephone service receiving referrals and offering counselling and advice on child protection matters. The NSPCC offers a range of services to children and their families. Its network of over 100 protection teams and projects undertake activities including investigations, assessment and therapeutic work, family care, training, consultation service to other child care professionals and specialist work.

Ockenden Venture: (See General Section)
Care for refugees

Parents Aid (Helping Families): Hare Street Family Centre, Harberts Road, Harlow, Essex CM19 0DJ
Tel: 01279 452166
Telephone advice for parents of children in care

Peper Harow Foundation: 14 Charterhouse Square, London EC1M 6AX   Tel: 0171 251 0672/6072
Projects for children with serious emotional and behavioural difficulties

Playgroup Network: PO Box 23, Whitley Bay, Tyne and Wear, NE26 3DB   Tel: 0191 252 1516
National network of playgroups and parent/toddler groups

Play Matters (National Association of Toy and Leisure Libraries): 68 Churchway, London NW1 1LT
Tel: 0171 387 9592

TAMBA (Twins and Multiple Births Association): PO Box 30, Little Sutton, South Wirral L66 1TH   Tel: 0151 348 0020
Advice and support to parents

Toy Aids (Educational Aids for Disabled Children):
Lodbourne Farm House, Lodbourne Green, Gillingham,
Dorset SP8 4EA Tel: 017476 2256

'Who Cares' Trust: Citybridge House, 235-245 Goswell
Road, Islington, London EC1V 7JD Tel: 0171 251 3117
Services to young people in care

WRVS Children's Holiday Scheme: 233-244 Stockwell
Road, London SW9 9SP Tel: 0171 733 3388

Children with special needs

AFASIC: 347 Central Markets, Smithfield, London
EC1A 9NH Tel: 0171 236 3632
Association for all speech-impaired children

Contact a Family: 16 Stratton Ground, London SW1P 2HP
Tel: 0171 383 3555
Self-help for families with disabled or ill children

Council for Disabled Children: 8 Wakley Street, Islington,
London EC1V 7QE Tel: 0171 842 6000, Fax: 0171 278 9512

Hyperactive Children's Support Group: 71 Whyke Lane,
Chichester, West Sussex PO Box 19 2LD Tel: 01903 725182
(Tues-Fri, 10am-3.30pm)

I CAN (Invalid Children's Aid): 1-3 Duffern Street,
London EC17 8NA Tel: 0171 374 4422, Fax: 0171 374 2762

Lady Hoare Trust for Physically Disabled Children: 4th
Floor, Mitre House, 44-46 Fleet Street, London EC4Y 1BN
Tel: 0171 583 1951

**National Association for the Welfare of Children in
Hospital:** Argyle House, 29-31 Euston Road, London
NW1 2SD Tel: 0171 833 2041

Voluntary Council for Handicapped Children: NCB,
8 Wakley Street, London EC1V 7QE Tel: 0171 267 5940

British Youth Council: 57 Chalton Street, London
NW1 1HU Tel: 0171 387 7559

Fairbridge: 5 Westminster Bridge Road, London SE1 7XW
Tel: 0171 928 1704
National charity for young people in inner cities

First Key (The National Leaving Care Advisory Service):
Head Office, Oxford Chambers, Oxford Place, Leeds
LS1 3AX Tel: 01132 443 8898

National Youth Agency: 17-23 Albion Street, Leicester
LE1 6GD Tel: 01533 471200

Disability and illness

Break: 20 Hooks Hill Road, Sheringham, Norfolk
NR26 8NL Tel: 01263 823170, Fax: 01263 825560
Holidays and respite care

British Sports Association for the Disabled (Head Office):
Mary Glen Haig Suite, 34 Osnaburgh Street, London
NW1 3ND Tel: 0171 383 7277

British Red Cross: 9 Grosvenor Crescent, London
SW1X 7EJ Tel: 0171 235 5454

**D.I.A.L. (National Association of Disablement Advice
and Information Lines):** Park Lodge, St Catherine's
Hospital, Tickhill Road, Doncaster DN4 8QN
Tel: 01302 310123

The Disability Information Trust: Mary Marlborough Lodge, Nuffield Orthopaedic Centre, Headington, Oxford OX3 7LD Tel: 01865 227592
Equipment for disabled people

Headway (National Head Injuries Association): 7 King Edward Court, King Edward Street, Nottingham NG1 1EW Tel: 01602 240800

Mobility Information Service: Unit 2A Atcham Estate, Upton Magna, Shrewsbury SY4 AUG Tel: 0174 375889

National Demonstration Centre: Pinderfields General Hospital, Wakefield WF1 4DG Tel: 01924 375217
Information and advice on disabled living

PHAB (Physically handicapped and able-bodied): 12-14 London Road, Croydon CR0 2TA Tel: 0181 667 9443

SKILL – National Bureau for Students with Disabilities: 336 Brixton Road, London SW9 7AA Tel: 0171 274 0565/7840, Minicom 0171 978 9890

SPOD (The Association to Aid the Sexual and Personal Relationships of People with a Disability): 286 Camden Road, London N7 0BJ Tel: 0171 607 8851/2

Wales Council for the Disabled: Llys Ifor, Crescent Road, Caerphilly, Mid Glamorgan CF8 1XL Tel: 01222 887325

Particular illnesses and disabilities

Alzheimer's Disease Society: Gordon House, 10 Greencoat Place, London SW1P 1PH Tel: 0171 306 0606

Arthritis and Rheumatism Council: Copeman House, St. Mary's Court, Chesterfield, Derbyshire S41 7TD Tel: 01246 558 007, Fax: 01246 558 007

Arthritis Care: 18 Stephenson Way, London NW1 2HD
Tel: 0171 916 1500/1505, Helpline: 0800 289170

Asthma Helpline: Tel: 01345 010203 (1-9pm, Mon-Fri)

British Diabetic Association: 10 Queen Anne Street,
London W1M 0BD Tel: 0171 323 1531

British Epilepsy Association: Anstey House, 40 Hanover
Square, Leeds LS3 1BE Tel: 01132 439393

National Information Centre: Tel: 01345 089599

British Heart Foundation: 14 Fitzhardinge Street, London
W1H 4DH Tel: 0171 935 0185

British Migraine Association: 178a High Road, Byfleet,
West Byfleet, Surrey KT14 7ED Tel: 01932 352468,
Fax: 01932 351257

Migraine Trust: 45 Great Ormond Street, London
WC1N 3HZ Tel: 0171 278 2676, Fax: 0171 831 5174

Chest, Heart and Stroke Association: CHSE House,
Whitecross Street, London EC1Y 9JJ Tel: 0171 490 7999,
Fax: 0171 490686

Mental Health Media Council: 380-384 Harrow Road,
London W9 2HU Tel: 0171 286 2346
Information/advice

MIND (National Association for Mental Health): Granta
House, 15-19 Broadway, London E15 4BQ
Tel: 0181 519 2122

Motor Neurone Disease Association: PO Box 246,
Northampton, NN1 2PR Tel: 01604 250 505

Multiple Sclerosis Society: 25 Effie Road, London
SW6 1EE Tel: 0171 736 6267

2A North Charlotte Street, Edinburgh, EH2 4HR
Tel: 0131 225 3600

Muscular Dystrophy Group: 7-11 Prescott Place, London
SW4 6BS Tel: 0171 720 8055, Fax: 0171 498 0670

National Aids Helpline: Tel: 0800 567 123

National Back Pain Association: 31-33 Park Road,
Teddington, Middlesex TW11 8ST Tel: 0181 977 5474

Parkinson's Disease Society: 2 Ivebury Court, 325 Latimer
Road, London W10 6RA Tel: 0171 383 3513

SANE: 2nd Floor, 199-206 Old Marylebone Road, London
Tel: 0171 724 6520

SANELINE: Helpline: 0171 724 8000 (2pm-midnight)

SCOPE – The Spastics Society: 12 Park Crescent, London
W1N 4EQ Tel: 0171 636 5020

Sensory disabilities

British Deaf Association: 38 Victoria Place, Carlisle,
Cumbria CA1 1HU Tel: 01228 28719, Minicom/Voice:
01228 48844, Fax: 01228 41420

Royal National Institute for the Deaf: Head Office,
19-23 Featherstone Street, London EC1Y 8SL
Tel: 0171 296 8000, Fax: 0171 296 8199

Royal National Institute for the Blind: 224 Great Portland Street, London W1N 6AA Tel: 0171 388 1266, Fax: 0171 388 2034

SENSE (National Deaf, Blind and Rubella Association): 11/13 Clifton Terrace, Finsbury Park, London N4 3SR Tel: 0171 272 7774, Fax: 0171 272 6612

Learning disabilities

BREAK: 20 Hooks Hill Road, Sheringham, Norfolk NR26 8NL Tel: 01263 823170
Holidays and respite care for children and adults

British Dyslexia Association: 98 London Road, Reading, Berkshire RG1 5AU Tel: 01734 668271 Fax: 01734 351927

British Institute of Learning Disabilities: Wolverhampton Road, Kidderminster, Worcestershire DY10 3PP Tel: 01562 850251 Fax: 01562 851970

CARE (for people with mental handicap): Head Office, 9 Weir Road, Kibworth, Leicester LE8 0LQ Tel: 0116 2793225, Fax: 0116 2796384

Down's Syndrome Association: 155 Mitcham Road, Tooting, London SW17 9PG Tel: 0181 682 4001, Fax: 0181 682 4012

Scottish Down's Syndrome Association: 158-160 Balgreen Road, Edinburgh EH11 3AU

ENABLE (Scottish Society for the Mentally Handicapped): 6th Floor, 7 Buchanan Street, Glasgow G1 3HZ Tel: 0141 226 4541, Fax: 0141 204 4395

MENCAP (Royal Society for Mentally Handicapped Children and Adults): 123 Golden Lane, London EC1 0RT Tel: 0171 454 0454, Fax: 0171 608 3254

National Autistic Society: 276 Willesden Lane, London NW2 5RB Tel: 0181 451 1114

UK Sports Association for People with Mental Handicap: 30 Philip Lane, Tottenham, London N15 4JB Tel: 0181 885 1177

The elderly

Age Concern, England: Astral House, 1268 London Road, London SW16 4ER Tel: 0181 679 8000

Age Concern, Scotland: 113 Rose Street, Edinburgh EC2 3DI Tel: 0131 220 3345, Fax: 0131 220 2779

Age Concern, Cymru: 1 Cathedral Road, Cardiff CF1 9SD Tel: 01222 371566, Fax: 01222 399562

Age Concern, Northern Ireland: 6 Lower Crescent, Belfast B17 1NR Tel: 01203 245729

Help the Aged: St James' Walk, London EC1R 0BE Tel: 0171 253 0253, Helpline: 0800 289404 (10am-4pm, Mon-Fri)

Addiction and dependency

ACCEPT (Addiction Community Centres for Education, Prevention and Treatment): 200 Seagrave Road, London SW16 1RQ Tel: 0171 381 3155

Alcohol Concern: 275 Grays Inn Road, London WC1X 8QF Tel: 0171 833 3471

Alcoholics Anonymous: Stonebow, York YO1 2NJ
Tel: 01904 644026/7/8/9

Alcohol Prevention and Counselling Service: 34 Electric
Lane, London SW9 8JT Tel: 0171 737 3570

Church of England National Council for Social Aid:
38 Ebury Street, London SW1 0LU Tel: 0171 730 6175

National Alcohol Helpline: Weddel House, 7th Floor,
13-14 West Smithfield, London EC1A 9DL Tel: 0171 332 0202

Drug dependency

ADFAM (Aid for Addicts and Families): 1st Floor, Chapel
House, Hatton Place, London EC1N 8ND Tel: 0171 405 3923

DAIS (Drugs Advice and Information Service): 38 West
Street, Brighton BN1 2RE Tel: 01273 21000

National Drugs Helpline: Main UK number (24 hours):
Tel: 0800 77 66 00; Wales: 0800 37 11 41 (10am-2am)

Release: 388 Old Street, London EC1V 9LT Tel: 0171 729 9904
Advice line: Mon-Fri, 10am-6pm; 24-hour emergency
helpline: 0171 603 8654
Information and advice for users, their friends and families

Smoking

ASH (Action on Smoking and Health): 109 Gloucester
Place, London W1H 3PH Tel: 0171 935 3519

Gambling

Gamblers Anonymous (support for compulsive gamblers); also GAMANON (for their families and friends): PO Box 88, London SW10 0EU. 24-hour helpline: 0181 741 4181

Services and help for offenders

Langley House Trust: General Secretary, 46 Market Square, Witney, Oxon OX8 6AL Tel: 01993 774075 / 778154
Accommodation and support for ex-offenders

National Association of Victim Support Schemes: 39 Brixton Road, London SW9 6DZ Tel: 0171 735 9166

Prisoners' Wives and Families Society: 254 Caledonian Road, Islington, London N1 Tel: 0171 278 3981

Acknowledgements

The prayer from *The Spiritual Exercise: A Literal Translation and a Contemporary Reading* by David L. Fleming is reproduced with the permission of The Institute of Jesuit Sources, St Louis, Missouri.

Unless otherwise stated, Scripture quotations taken from the *Holy Bible, New International Version*. Copyright © 1973, 1978, 1984 by International Bible Society. Used by permission of Hodder & Stoughton Ltd. All rights reserved. 'NIV' is a registered trademark of International Bible Society. UK trademark number 1448790.

Where stated, Scripture quotations taken from *The New Jerusalem Bible* published and © Copyright 1985 by Darton Longman & Todd Ltd and Doubleday & Co Inc. and used by permission of the publisher.

Notes